Original title:
Rooted in Rhyme

Copyright © 2025 Creative Arts Management OÜ
All rights reserved.

Author: Julian Montgomery
ISBN HARDBACK: 978-1-80566-591-5
ISBN PAPERBACK: 978-1-80566-876-3

Whispers of the Earth

The ground below starts to hum,
As worms dance to a rhythmic drum.
With every squish and sludgy sound,
The nature's jokes are all around.

Ants wear hats and march in line,
Their little feet a tap of time.
While daisies giggle in the breeze,
And tease the bees with silly sneeze.

From Soil to Sound

In silt and mud where whispers play,
The cucumbers sing at the end of the day.
Tomatoes boast of their blushy red,
While carrots joke from their leafy bed.

A potato rolls a pun so round,
With laughter echoing from the ground.
The roots all chuckle, they know the score,
Life's better with a little uproar.

Verses Beneath the Surface

Below the grass, the rhymes align,
As tulips wax their fancy shine.
A dandelion tells a tale,
Of windy days and autumn gales.

The soil spills secrets, hear them giggle,
As earthworms twist and give a wiggle.
The mushrooms laugh, they're quite absurd,
In silly hats, they're rarely heard.

Ties that Bind in Verse

The roots engage in silly fights,
Pulling pranks on summer nights.
With tendrils wrapped in a playful twist,
No one's left out; they all insist.

With echoes through the leafy dome,
They sing a chorus, call it home.
And in the dark, the critters cheer,
For fun in rhyme is always near.

The Chorus of the Clovers

In a patch where the clovers sway,
The ants put on a show each day.
They dance and twirl in the sun,
While giggling, oh what fun!

A ladybug leads with flair,
While grasshoppers leap through the air.
The bumblebees buzz in delight,
Creating music from morning to night.

Frogs croak a bass line so deep,
While nearby, the daisies peep.
The whole meadow joins in one tune,
A melody that makes us swoon.

So come join this merry affair,
With clovers laughing without a care.
Together we sing, our hearts so bold,
In this garden, joy unfolds.

Lyrical Landscapes

A valley of verses, so bright and wide,
Where turtles race and snails glide.
The sun spins tales with each warm ray,
As flowers choose their dance today.

In every stroke of the painter's hand,
A valley sings, a whimsical land.
With wildflowers crafting a unique beat,
While squirrels tap dance with nimble feet.

The hills wear hats of cloud and sun,
Creating giggles as they run.
With echoes of laughter on gentle breeze,
Even the rocks wear smiles with ease.

So wander through these lively scenes,
Where life leans in with playful dreams.
In landscapes filled with quirky sights,
Join the fun and share the lights!

Whispers from the Wild

In the woods where secrets breathe,
The trees tell tales beneath their leaves.
A fox wearing socks shares a grin,
While the owl hoots out a joke to begin.

Mice hold meetings in the tall grass,
Plotting pranks as the moments pass.
With acorns bouncing like little balls,
Echoing laughter through woodland halls.

A raccoon bumbling in a hat,
Finds it hard to catch that pesky rat.
While the butterflies spin tales of delight,
In a world where mischief takes flight.

So listen close, embrace the wild,
For every creature has a story compiled.
With whispers that tingle the tips of your ears,
Come join in the charm that brings cheerful cheers.

In the Heart of the Orchard

In the heart of the orchard, apples sway,
As bees buzz with jokes throughout the day.
The trees wear aprons, all set to bake,
Creating laughter with every shake.

The pears roll for a bid at charm,
While the grapes giggle, ripe and warm.
Cherries chuckle as they dangle high,
Dropping puns with a cherry pie.

A rabbit hops in, top hat in tow,
Hosting a party, stealing the show.
With every sip of nectar so sweet,
They find themselves dancing on tiny feet.

So pluck a fruit and join the spree,
In this orchard joke fest, wild and free.
Beneath the boughs where laughter grows,
Join the fun that nature bestows.

Inked in the Undergrowth

In shadows thick with leafy cheer,
A squirrel's dance brings giggles near.
With acorn hats and twirls so spry,
They form a band beneath the sky.

The mushrooms nod, they join the song,
In mismatched socks, they prance along.
The wind whispers jokes through the trees,
While ants march on with silly ease.

A rabbit with a wink and grin,
Plays hopscotch with a hesitant pin.
He trips, he flips, he's quite the sight,
As ladybugs cheer with all their might.

In this lush space, where laughter grows,
Every leaf knows the giggle flows.
Where roots and rhymes in chaos play,
And every critter finds their way.

Ballads of the Burgeoning

A tangle of stems in a vibrant mess,
The flowers argue who's the best dress.
One claims blue is the color for kings,
While the daisies shout, 'We're queens of spring!'

With bees in chorus, buzzing their tune,
They debate over flowers from morning to noon.
"Your pollen's too sweet, I don't like the taste!"
Cried a stubborn bloom, in stupor and haste.

The carrots below, in a bed made of dirt,
Giggled at squash with his bright yellow shirt.
"I'm stylish," said squash, with a pumpkin's pride,
While radishes rolled with glee by the side.

This garden full of chortles and chaff,
Makes weeds feel like they're the ones to laugh.
With roots intertwined, they share their jest,
Finding joy in the verdant fest.

The Cadence of Climbing Vines

With tendrils twirling like a dance,
Vines whisper secrets, given a chance.
One wraps 'round a tree, feeling divine,
While another just wants to sip on some wine.

They argue about who's the best climber,
Poking fun at the ivy, the great and the minor.
"Look at me twist, I'm the reigning champ!"
While the other yells, "You're a leafy old lamp!"

The sun breaks bright, it's a perfect day,
For a giggly game of tug-of-war play.
They scale, they slip, they nearly topple,
Yet fumble with grace, there's always a wobble.

So let them climb and stretch and weave,
In this viney realm where all believe.
That laughter's the root of the fun they find,
Winding and twirling, quite unconfined.

Rooted in Resonance

In the garden of giggles, we plant our jokes,
Where puns bloom brightly like colorful folks.
Laughter spills out like watering cans,
Each chuckle a sprout in our comedy plans.

We dance with the weeds, those sly little creeps,
Tickling our toes while the whole world sleeps.
Paths lined with humor grow taller and teeter,
Who knew that a smile would grow much sweeter?

Beneath the old oak, we gather and tease,
Sipping on punch made from humor and breeze.
With roots in the soil, we dig up the fun,
And share hearty laughs until day is done.

Reflection in Reflection

A mirror can't laugh, but boy, it can smirk,
With faces that twist – oh, the funny quirks!
Shadows of antics who play hide and seek,
We crack up so much, we can barely speak.

In the pond of our thoughts, ducks paddle with ease,
While fish swim in circles, just aiming to tease.
Reflections give back every giggle we find,
So we splash a bit harder, leaving no laugh behind.

The ripples of humor, they bounce and they play,
Creating a chorus of nonsense each day.
In this silly funhouse, we dart to and fro,
Finding smiles in ripples, making laughter grow!

The Shade of Forgotten Stories

Underneath the old tree, where secrets reside,
Whispers of mischief and laughter collide.
Squirrels tell tales with a nutty little twist,
While raccoons roll by, oh, they can't be missed!

In the shade of those stories, we gather to share,
A circus of fables from everywhere.
Mice on a tightrope, a cat in a hat,
Each tale paints a picture, a whimsical spat.

A picnic of nonsense, we feast on delight,
With cupcakes of giggles and jokes taking flight.
Forgotten canaries sing songs after dark,
In this shade of stories, we leave our mark.

Poetic Growth

From seeds of laughter, our verses take root,
Each line like a branch, each rhyme like a shoot.
Silly words sprout with a twist and a cheer,
As the garden of humor keeps thriving right here.

With sunshine of giggles and rain of delight,
We dance through the stanzas, all day and night.
The soil's full of puns, just waiting to bloom,
Growing tall with each chuckle that brightens the room.

In the orchard of rhymes, we swing and we sway,
Harvesting laughter from dawn until gray.
The flora of fun, oh so wild and so free,
In this plot of poetic, we all plant the glee!

Underneath the Umbrella

Raindrops dance like silly feet,
While ducks in boots skip down the street.
A cat with shades lounges in split,
Sipping tea, oh what a fit!

The umbrella's got secrets to spill,
It's hosting a party, a jolly thrill.
With penguins waltzing and frogs in ties,
The colors burst like candy pies!

Whirlwind Words

Words fly around like buzzing bees,
Tickling noses, rustling leaves.
A squirrel named Bob starts to rhyme,
And suddenly, it feels like prime!

With puns that leap and jokes that glide,
They twist and twirl, just like a ride.
Giggling gophers join the spree,
Singing verses in wild jubilee!

Verses in the Vine

Vines twist tales in a frisky way,
While grapes gossip about their day.
A ladybug's laugh rolls down the vine,
Tickling the toes of a dancing pine.

The sun beams in with a silly grin,
A waltz on leaves, and let's begin!
Cherries cheer, oh what a scene,
In this orchard, life's a dream!

Stanzas of the Soil

In the soil, the worms have a show,
Wiggling 'round with a flair for flow.
They rhyme with roots, they bounce and jive,
In this earthy stage, all come alive!

The daisies clap with petals bright,
While beetles tap in pure delight.
With laughter sprouting like dancehall tunes,
The garden life booms with cartoons!

Cadence of the Canopy

Up above the trees, they sway,
Leaves dancing, come what may.
Squirrels sing a silly tune,
Skipping sunlight, playing noon.

Branches hold a jolly crowd,
Where the chirps are loud and proud.
A parrot steals the show each time,
Wings flapping to the beat of rhyme.

Nuts and berries in a pie,
Sipped with laughter, oh my my!
Bouncing branches, joyfully shake,
Nature's stage, a grand mistake.

When the wind comes through the place,
All the critters join the race.
Leafy laughter fills the air,
In the canopy, none to spare.

Trails of Inspiration

Hiking paths that twist and twine,
Every corner, jokes align.
Raccoons peek with knowing grins,
As each step brings giggles, wins.

Mushrooms pop like little caps,
Telling stories of mishaps.
Nature's art on every trail,
Wacky wonders, set to sail.

Bouncing boulders, slippery shoes,
Forest whispers, playful blues.
Every footstep's full of fun,
Running wild, we all just run.

With each turn, a laugh prevails,
Chasing shadows, telling tales.
Embrace the joy, the playful quest,
Inspiration dwells with zest.

Melodic Mycelium

Beneath the ground, where tales unfold,
Fungi giggle, stories told.
Spreading spores like silly seeds,
In a dance, they meet their needs.

Mushrooms march with playful grace,
Mimicking a funny face.
Underneath the leafy cover,
Mycelium, a hidden lover.

Growing networks, sly and sly,
Connecting life as time goes by.
With roots entwining in a race,
Jokes and puns in every space.

Making friends in darkest night,
Critters laugh in pure delight.
Fungi sing a tune so sweet,
Nature's secrets, a forest beat.

The Rhythm of the Rain

Pitter-patter on the ground,
Raindrops happily abound.
Laughter fills the stormy sky,
Dancing drops as they fly by.

Puddles form a shimmering stage,
Splashing joy at every age.
Umbrellas twirl in silly flight,
Chasing clouds that hide from light.

Drenched with giggles, people cheer,
Every drop's a little dear.
Wet and wild, the world revives,
In the rain, the fun derives.

Moody clouds may seem so gray,
But they're just here to play.
As long as water's in the game,
We dance and laugh without the shame.

Fables of the Foliage

In the forest, leaves do chatter,
Squirrels gamble, climbing up the ladder.
Mushrooms dance in their fanciest hats,
While wise old owls give silly spats.

Bunnies hop, they trip and tumble,
While ants in line just laugh and grumble.
Trees gossip about the passing breeze,
Wondering where it hid the cheese!

Rabbits joke about carrot stew,
As the flowers giggle in morning dew.
Nature's stage is a comical sight,
Each creature here feels just right.

So when you stroll through leafy lanes,
Join the laughter, forget the pains.
For in this land of silly seams,
Lies a world woven with funny dreams.

Verses of the Vines

Vines waltz around the garden gate,
Joking with flowers about their fate.
Tomatoes laugh as they grow so round,
While cucumbers slide without a sound.

Grapes gossip, hanging in the sun,
Saying, 'Life is great, oh what fun!'
But then a pickle joins the fray,
'You think that's funny? Just wait till May!'

Bees buzz jokes about the honey fly,
While pumpkins grin as they grow high.
But watch the squash, they like to tease,
Making pies that bring you to your knees!

In this garden full of whimsy vibes,
Laughter's contagious, it thrives and thrives.
Join the party, grab a seat,
Where vines are jolly and life's a treat.

Nourished by Nature

Under the sun, the radishes giggle,
Spinning tales with every wiggle.
Carrots wear shades, feeling real cool,
While lettuces lounge, all chill by the pool.

The corn stalks sway, playing a game,
'Who can grow taller? That's the aim!'
While berries blush as they ripen in rows,
Cracking jokes that only nature knows.

The daisies burst in spontaneous cheer,
Sharing secrets that only they hear.
And on the breeze, a laughterless song,
'This is our place; it's where we belong!'

So come and taste the puns on your plate,
In a world where flavor and humor await.
Nourished by laughter, life becomes bright,
In each delicious bite, there's pure delight.

Serenade of the Seeds

Seeds gather round for a nightly tale,
Arguing if it's spring or a snail.
One sprout shouts, 'I'm the cutest around!'
While others roll over, giggling, confound.

Little acorns boast of their might,
'I'm destined to grow into a tree, just right!'
While the daisies chime in, singing away,
'We are the stars of this nature ballet!'

In the dark, they whisper of dreams in soil,
Plots of mischief and nurturing toil.
Twirling 'round in their fluffy bed,
Creating laughter with seeds in their head.

So let the garden music fill up your mind,
With quirky rhythms and laughter combined.
For in this serenade of joy and creed,
Each little giggle is a wondrous seed.

Nature's Quiet Chorus

In the woods, the squirrels chatter,
Telling tales of nuts that matter.
The birds just giggle in their trees,
While ants march on with humorous ease.

Frogs croak out a symphony,
Pond rippling with their harmony.
A raccoon laughs at a rolling log,
As time flows by like a playful fog.

Deer prance with an awkward dance,
While bunnies hop in a silly prance.
The flowers sway, they seem to giggle,
As bees buzz by in a joyful wiggle.

Thus nature sings its quirky tune,
Under the light of the bright full moon.
A chorus formed of funny friends,
Where laughter lives and never ends.

The Measure of the Meadow

In fields where daisies sway and spin,
The grass tickles toes and makes them grin.
A quirky breeze begins to tease,
As butterflies float with effortless ease.

The daisies whisper, 'Count us wrong,'
'For we're more than just a flowery throng!'
A dandelion, proud like a king,
Says, 'I've got more seeds than you can sing!'

Under the sun, the insects prance,
Determined to join in the hopscotch dance.
A snail enters, takes it real slow,
While ants say, "Whoa, where did you go?"

With every bloom, laughter ignites,
In the meadow, the humor excites.
Nature's math is fun and bright,
A joyful explosion of pure delight.

Harmonies from the Hearth

In the kitchen, pots begin to clatter,
While cats skitter by in a futile patter.
The old dog snores with a chuckle and sigh,
As the kettle sings a high-pitched cry.

Flour flies when kids make a mess,
Hands covered in dough, oh what a stress!
The bread rises high, but then it pops,
Little giggles escape from the chops.

Mom shouts, "Dinner's ready, all!"
The taste of chaos in food's great sprawl.
As cupcakes melt, it's a culinary game,
Where everyone laughs, but none take the blame.

So flavors mingle, sweet and sour,
Laughter reigns in the cooking hour.
Together they stir with joyful hearts,
Harmonic fun in all their arts.

Chants of the Seasons

When spring rolls in, the frogs start to sing,
Inviting joy, on the wings of a spring.
Blossoms burst forth in giggles and cheer,
As bees buzz along, with nothing to fear.

Summer winks, and the sun plays a tune,
Kids splash in puddles, making smiles bloom.
Ice cream drips down with a silly flop,
While fireflies twinkle, never want to stop.

Autumn arrives with a crunchy delight,
Leaves dance around, what a colorful sight!
Pumpkins roll in, wearing goofy grins,
As harvest time brings out the giggly wins.

Then winter comes in with a frosty laugh,
Snowflakes tumble, it's a fun little path.
Hot cocoa flows with marshmallows so round,
Seasons bring joy in each silly sound.

Rhythm of the Roiling Earth

Beneath the soil, the worms do jig,
With tiny hats and a makeshift gig.
The beetles cheer, as ants take flight,
A waltz of critters in morning light.

The rocks keep time with a thudding beat,
While squirrels tap dance on dainty feet.
Mushrooms mingle in polka dress,
Oh what a mess, it's anyone's guess!

The daisies sway in a breezy spin,
While frogs croak loud, let the fun begin.
The trees join in with a rustling cheer,
A symphony of life we all hold dear.

So laugh along with this earthy tune,
Where nature plays, the sun and moon.
In every nook, or tree, or fern,
There's a rhythm waiting for us to learn.

Ancestral Echoes

In the attic lurks my great-granddad,
He tells his tales, oh they're never sad.
With a wink and a nudge, he twists his mustache,
At grandma's old pot—just throw in some trash!

The echoes giggle, as stories unfold,
Of silly socks and beans that turned cold.
Uncle Joe's lost in a sock puppet fight,
While a ghost tells jokes that just might be right!

Ceramics clatter as memories crash,
In a game of charades, you're sure to splash.
A wink from the pictures that line the wall,
For every stumble, we'll have a ball!

So let's raise a glass to the tales of yore,
As laughter and whimsy forever soar.
With each silly story that we retell,
Ancestral echoes ring like a bell.

The Weave of the Wilderness

In the forest, the branches twirl,
With squirrels doing a wacky whirl.
The flowers roll in a grassy spree,
While a raccoon plays on the old TV!

The river hums a catchy tune,
As frogs join in—what a croaky boon!
Trees stretch high like a grand parade,
While bees buzz in a jazzy charade.

On the rocks, a turtle strikes a pose,
With a fashionable hat, nobody knows.
The ferns are spinning like disco balls,
Oh what a party, hear those calls!

So venture forth into nature's fun,
Where every creature dances under the sun.
In the weave of life, let laughter bloom,
In the wilderness, there's always room!

Cacophony of Colors

In a garden bright, the colors clash,
With purple peacocks making a splash.
Red ants march in a line so bold,
While yellow daisies claim to be gold.

A cacophony bright, the hues collide,
As rainbow fish take a joyful ride.
Green frogs croak in their finest attire,
While butterflies twirl in a wild choir!

The sunbeams giggle as clouds play coy,
Pink kittens chase after a floppy toy.
In this wild world, where colors thrive,
A splash of whimsy helps us survive!

So paint the day with laughter and cheer,
In this vibrant chaos, draw everyone near.
In a garden alive, let your spirit dance,
For the magic of color is quite the romance!

Unheard Elegies

In a garden, weeds have dreams,
They plot and scheme in leafy teams.
With daisies rolling eyes so sly,
They laugh at roses passing by.

A sunflower boasts it's the best,
While tulips giggle, less than blessed.
The lettuce sings a woeful tune,
Regrets it missed the dance under the moon.

Chirping crickets join the show,
With grasshoppers putting on a toe.
The wind it whispers jokes untold,
As nature plots mischief, brave and bold.

So here's to blooms in every hue,
Who dream of stardom, just like you.
In petals soft, their humor beams,
As echoes frown on earthly themes.

The Silent Symphony

In the woods, where silence sways,
With squirrels conducting grand displays.
A symphony of silent sights,
As trees hum tunes on starry nights.

The mushrooms dance a jolly jig,
Each twirl a sign, each flick a gig.
The brook's a flute, the wind, a drum,
It seems the nature's quite funsome.

The owl hoots jokes in night's cool air,
While crickets play without a care.
Together join in harmony,
In a rhythm catchy as can be.

So grab your friends, a leafy crew,
And laugh along with me and you.
For in this silence, joy shall bloom,
In every shadow, there's a room.

Aria of the Arbor

The trees perform their grand ballet,
With branches swaying in a play.
The roots all giggle underground,
As whispers float from bush to bound.

The flowers waltz with vibrant glee,
In colors bright, they're wild and free.
A bumblebee starts singing low,
While ants parade all in a row.

A squirrel's leap, a funny twist,
The sunbeams join the evening list.
As laughter echoes through the leaves,
The trees hold secrets none believes.

So hum along, dear friend of mine,
In every branch, there's joy to find.
The winds will carry, take a chance,
Join nature's grand, hilarious dance.

The Network of the Natural

In the realm where green things grow,
Each critter's got a tale to show.
The ants in suits, they've planned the day,
With secret codes in leafy play.

The daisies gossip all around,
With tulips tilting, so profound.
They trade their best and worst of woes,
With violets blushing, that's how it goes.

The trees hold meetings, wise and grand,
As breezes whisper, lend a hand.
Caterpillars plot their flights,
While spiders weave their comical sights.

So join this dance, in nature's sphere,
With every chuckle, bring us cheer.
The network laughs, entwined in time,
Creating joy, beyond the rhyme.

Blooms and Ballads

In the garden, weeds dance high,
Singing tunes that make us sigh.
Sunflowers gossip, roses tease,
While daisies giggle in the breeze.

The carrots wear a hat of green,
Chanting rhymes like they've seen.
Radishes roll and potatoes prance,
This is quite the veggie dance!

Grounded Melodies

The soil hums a silly song,
Where worms wiggle all day long.
The daisies laugh at the bumblebee,
'Thinks he's busy, poor guy, can't you see?'

Underneath a leaf so bright,
A snail races with delight.
While ants march on their own parade,
In this ground of fun, they never fade.

The Pulse of the Ground

Beneath the earth, the critters scream,
Playing hide and seek, what a dream!
Moles are sneaky, quick on their feet,
While grasshoppers sing and tap to the beat.

The roots do cha-cha through the dirt,
Wiggling slow, in their little skirt.
Each rock joins in, in a clumsy way,
Creating a jam that's here to stay!

Harvesting Harmony

The pumpkins plan a big parade,
While corn husks giggle, unafraid.
Tomatoes blush, they're dressed so grand,
Squash struts by, they clap their hand.

With every pick and every cheer,
The fruit and veg make it clear.
Harvest time brings laughter loud,
A merry feast to make us proud!

Unfolding in Silken Syllables

Words like noodles dance and twirl,
They slip and slide, give them a whirl.
Each phrase a twist, a silly spree,
A playful way to rhyme with glee.

When laughter meets the page so bright,
Each pun a spark, a pure delight.
With every chuckle, lines unwind,
A tapestry of fun, we find.

The rhythm sways like birds in flight,
As verses twist and turn just right.
In silken whispers, they take shape,
A giggle here, a rhyme to drape.

So join this dance, let laughter sing,
With every line, new joy we bring.
For in this play of words we see,
The lighter side of poetry.

Roots of Rapture

In gardens lush, where puns take hold,
Each line a story, brightly told.
The flowers giggle, the bugs join in,
A riot of sound, where laughs begin.

The soil beneath is rich with cheer,
With every word, the joy draws near.
Roots stretching deep, they tug and pull,
While metaphors dance and hearts feel full.

Under the sun, the verses sway,
Like leaves in breeze, they giggle away.
A playful poke at life's own jest,
Inviting all to join this fest.

So let us frolic, let us play,
In verses bright, we'll find our way.
For laughter grows where puns abound,
In rhymes of joy, true love is found.

The Sylvan Songbook

In woods where words begin to roam,
The trees hum tunes that feel like home.
Leaves rustle soft, in laughter's wake,
A melody, make no mistake.

Birds chirp in quips, a jovial choir,
Each bark a joke, a playful fire.
The branches sway, in rhymes they play,
Chasing the clouds, keeping gloom at bay.

With lightened hearts, we march along,
Singing together, a silly song.
In this songbook, joy unfurls,
A symphony of jests and swirls.

So grab your pen, let's sing and write,
In nature's lap, everything feels right.
For in these woods where laughter bounces,
The love of words forever flounces.

Where Metaphors Take Root

Amidst the muck, where jesters grow,
Metaphors laugh in the afterglow.
Each turn of phrase, a silly tease,
Whispers of joy dance in the breeze.

In patches bright, ideas sprout,
Like weeds of wit, they twist about.
The flowers bloom with quirky wit,
A garden filled with every bit.

With every phrase that we compose,
Laughter blooms like a joyous rose.
Digging deep for humor's prize,
In fertile soils, our joy will rise.

So come and play, don't be aloof,
Join in the fun, hop on the roof!
For where we plant our silly dreams,
Is where the laughter loudly beams.

The Dance of the Dandelions

In fields where the dandelions sway,
They jig and they prance all day.
With fluffy heads and seeds for hire,
They spread their giggles, they never tire.

A breeze blows by, they spin around,
Their laughter echoes, oh what a sound!
Each fluffy puff, a cheer so bright,
As they twirl and leap, a comical sight.

They challenge the winds, they play tag,
With every gust, their spirits brag.
Beneath the sun, in yellow gowns,
These loony flowers wear crown-like crowns.

So here's to the dandelions sweet,
With their silly moves and happy feet.
In a world where laughter grows,
They dance through life, as everybody knows!

Ballads of the Branches

In the treetops, branches croon,
Singing ballads to the moon.
They twist and twirl in comedic glee,
Each knot and twist, a melody free.

With every sway, they tell a tale,
Of windy days and mischievous gales.
A branch once slipped, fell for a bird,
And sang a song that was utterly absurd.

Leaves join in, with rustling laughs,
Each fluttering note, a goofy half.
The sun peeks down, with a playful grin,
For nature's joy is where it begins.

So let the branches sing out loud,
In a symphony of the silly and proud.
For in their tunes, we find the rhyme,
Of laughter wrapped in nature's time!

Resounding with the Rainfall

The rain drums down, a playful beat,
Puddles join in, oh what a treat!
Each droplet's tap, a funny sound,
As they dance on rooftops all around.

With splashes big, and splashes small,
The raindrops giggle, they have a ball.
They trickle down, like silly streams,
Leading to laughter and joyful dreams.

A frog leaps high, with a wetty croak,
Doing the cha-cha, what a joke!
While ducks glide by, in choreographed fun,
Beneath the clouds, they all outdone.

So let it pour, and let it play,
For a rainy dance upon the gray.
With every drop, the world comes alive,
In the rhythm of raindrops, we thrive!

Ode to the Old Oak

An old oak stands, with wisdom grand,
Its branches stretch like a giant hand.
With acorns dropped, a comedic mess,
Nature's jester, it's truly a bless.

Its bark is rough, with stories to share,
Of squirrels that dance without a care.
It whispers jokes to the bees and bugs,
In twisted humor and nature hugs.

The leaves applaud when the wind passes by,
Each rustle and crackle, a heartfelt sigh.
Oh, the tales it tells to the stars at night,
A legend of laughter, in the moonlight.

So here's to the oak, with its gnarled ways,
A funny old friend throughout the days.
In its wise embrace, we find a home,
Where giggles grow, and spirits roam!

The Soil's Soft Sonnet

In the garden, a chicken sings,
Among the flowers, it flaps its wings.
Worms do the cha-cha on the ground,
While bees buzz by in silly rounds.

Gnomes argue over who should mow,
While daisies play peekaboo in a row.
A rabbit's hat tricks make us laugh,
As carrots giggle, what a photograph!

The sunbeam tango lights the scene,
With dancing shades of tangerine.
The soil chuckles, soft and deep,
While daisies sway and wiggle, not sleep!

A snail with shades takes it slow,
Doing the limbo, stealing the show.
Nature gleefully ticks away,
In this garden, come laugh and play!

Interwoven in Imagery

A butterfly trips on its own flair,
While a squirrel declares it's a dare.
Pansies whisper jokes, oh so sly,
As ivy struts by with a wink in its eye.

The sky wears a hat made of fluff,
While clouds giggle, this is enough!
A bumblebee dances, stumbles, spins,
While daisies clap, wishing it wins.

The sun dips low, taking a bow,
And shadows break into a how-now-bow.
Frogs croak out their serenade,
As jokes in the breeze are carefully laid.

A raccoon with socks plays the flute,
As we laugh at this amusing hoot.
Every leaf rustles with mirth,
In this wild, whimsical earth!

The Tapestry of Time

Clock hands giggle as they spin,
Chasing shadows, trying to win.
A ticklish breeze nips at our toes,
As daisies twirl in lovely bows.

A wise old tree tells a silly tale,
Of squirrels on kayaks, setting sail.
Each leaf snaps jokes of days long past,
With laughter ringing, oh so fast!

Flowers wear time like a silly hat,
While bees buzz by, flapping their spat.
The sun blinks twice, what a sight,
As stars prepare for an evening flight.

Pebbles play chess, the rabbits compete,
As petals toss confetti, oh so sweet.
Every tick and tock, a chuckle's rhyme,
We dance through the fabric of time!

Notes from the Nurtured

In a corner, roots hold a concert,
Where carrots play drums, dressed quite assert.
A spinach sings tenor, leafy and bold,
While potatoes dance, oh, if they were sold!

Gifts of laughter fill the air,
Pumpkins juggle, without a care.
Each sprout takes a solo, wiggly and keen,
As nature's orchestra fills the scene.

The soil claps with a cheerful cheer,
Worms are the bouncers, never a fear.
The moon moonwalks, a curious sight,
As stars join in, what pure delight!

Laughter echoes through leafy lanes,
And the sun smiles wide, oh what gains!
In this garden of humor, we find our tune,
Making music beneath the afternoon!

Ties that Bind in Stanzas

In the garden of verses, we trip and we fall,
With rhymes on our shoes, we dance through it all.
A pun on a pun, oh what a delight,
Each stanza a giggle, a whiff of moonlight.

Twisted in laughter, we wiggle and rhyme,
Our brains doing somersaults, a nutty climb.
With ties made of laughter, we frolic and play,
In this wacky embrace, we're silly all day.

Deep in the Grove

Under leafy canopies, where acorns do fall,
We share silly stories, we giggle and sprawl.
With squirrels as our audience, and roots as our friends,
We rhyme like crazy, and hope it won't end.

The trees hum a tune, a silly old song,
While we tell our tall tales, and giggle along.
With breezes that tickle and shadows that sway,
In this funky old grove, we laugh every day.

Harmonies of the Heartstrings

A ukulele strums, what a jolly old sound,
As we stumble and bumble, all quaintly profound.
With heartstrings entwined in a jumble of giggles,
We craft a fine tune with our wacky little wiggles.

Rhymes bouncing off walls, like popcorn on cue,
We're spinning in circles, what else can we do?
With laughter our anthem, we sing loud and bright,
In this silly symphony, everything feels right.

Beneath the Canopy of Words

Beneath this great cover, we spin silly tales,
With words as our treasures, we sail in our gales.
From giggles to cackles, we cheerfully weave,
In this fabric of fun, it's hard to believe.

Our laughter like raindrops, it splashes around,
In puddles of puns, our glee knows no bound.
With banter like bees, buzzing joyfully here,
Underneath this word canopy, we shed every fear.

Choral Canopy

In a forest where squirrels sing,
Their voices twirl like a spring.
Beneath the branches, the laughter flows,
As dancing leaves put on a show.

Frogs join in with a croak or two,
While worms groove beneath, it's true.
The trees, they sway in perfect time,
Nature's joy in a comical mime.

Birds wear hats made of bright old leaves,
Each chirp a giggle, nobody grieves.
The sun shines down, a spotlight beam,
In this woodland ballet, we dream.

Laughter spills from trunk to bough,
Every bark has a silly vow.
With all the fun the woods can yield,
Who knew a tree could make you squealed?

The Bound of the Understory

In shadows deep, where giggles loom,
Fungi practice stand-up in the gloom.
Toadstools chuckle, it's quite a sight,
While crickets joke in the pale moonlight.

The owls make puns, they're quite the hoot,
Swaying softly in their feathered suit.
A hedgehog wears a tie made of moss,
He twirls and spins, oh what a boss!

The bramble bushes burst with glee,
Tickling each critter dancing free.
Beneath the vines, a merry crew,
Crafting chaos in the damp dew.

In this tangled, funny little land,
Life serves humor from nature's hand.
Each timid heart within the trees,
Find joy and laughter with the breeze.

Crown of the Canopy

Up above where the tall trees play,
Chirping jokes in a leafy way.
The canopy's crown with all its pride,
Houses a talent show inside.

With acorns tossed like little balls,
The woodland critters answer calls.
From treetop heights, the humor flies,
As raccoons pull their funny ties.

Squirrels juggle nuts with ease,
While chipmunks dance, it's sure to please.
The jests up high, oh what a scene,
In this leafy realm, we laugh and preen.

The sun dips low, the laughter rings,
As nature's orchestra plays funny things.
From crown to roots, a joyful spree,
In every rustle, humor's key.

Whispers in the Willow

Beneath the whispers of the trees,
Witty winks float on the breeze.
The willows laugh, their branches sway,
Sharing secrets of the day.

A frog in a tux wades through the stream,
Flashing a smile, living the dream.
The dragonflies dance with shimmery grace,
While a grumpy crow makes a funny face.

With rustling leaves, the trees conspire,
To spread their jokes and light the fire.
Each breeze a giggle, each droop a sigh,
In this nature's stage, watch humor fly.

The bark tells tales of chuckles past,
While shadows play, they flicker fast.
In this willow grove, a jovial tale,
Where laughter grows like a sweet, soft gale.

Verses in the Verdant Veil

In a garden where giggles grow,
Silly daisies dance to and fro.
Laughter sprouts beneath the sun,
Every petal tells a pun.

Worms wear hats, it's quite the sight,
Wiggling to the left and right.
A tulip sneezes, bless its bloom,
While bunnies hop and sweep the room.

Jokes erupt like bubbles in air,
Leaves trade stories with flair and care.
The sun winks down with a playful grin,
While the harvest of joy begins again.

Stanzas Sprouting from the Earth

A broccoli tree stands tall and proud,
With whispers echoing from the crowd.
Carrots giggle beneath the ground,
As funny faces can be found.

Radishes tell tales of their yore,
How they rolled and laughed, oh what a chore!
Peas get together for a playful scheme,
They dream of veggies in a marvelous dream.

Up above, a pumpkin king reigns,
With laughter echoing through the lanes.
In this patch, no frown remains,
Just goofy jokes in joyful chains.

Cadences of the Cosmos

Stars giggle in the midnight sway,
Planets play tag while comets play.
A moonbeam chuckles, lighting the night,
As galaxies swirl in sheer delight.

Saturn's rings spin tales of fun,
While Mars laughs loud beneath the sun.
Jupiter jests with a grin so wide,
Creating jokes on a cosmic ride.

Asteroids bounce with exuberant glee,
Winking at Earth, come laugh with me.
In the vastness, humor does thrive,
In the universe, it's joy that survives.

Harmonized in Hallowed Ground

Underneath the oak tree's shade,
Squirrels chatter, deals are made.
A rabbit with glasses reads a book,
While the wise old crow takes a nook.

The daisies gossip in frilly gowns,
Sharing secrets of silly clowns.
A fox tells jokes, crafting some cheer,
In this woodland, laughter is near.

The brook giggles as it trickles down,
Tickling toes of creatures in town.
In this space where humor is found,
Every heart is joyfully bound.

Songs of the Sylvan

In the woods where the critters play,
A squirrel claims the top of the hay.
He dances with glee, what a sight,
While birds laugh at him in flight.

A rabbit hops with a springy bound,
Cracking jokes without making a sound.
The trees snicker, the leaves join in,
As shadows wiggle, twirl, and spin.

A fox tells tales of grand charades,
While a turtle brags of his escapades.
Nature's punchlines float through the air,
In this forest, there's humor to spare.

So come join the fun, let laughter ring,
In the heart of the woods, where the wild things sing.
With a giggle, a wiggle, and a chortle or two,
In songs of the sylvan, there's joy just for you.

The Lyrical Landing

At the pond where the frogs tell time,
A chorus echoes, quite the rhyme.
One croaks loud, another whispers low,
As dragonflies join the feathery show.

A duck waddles in, with flair so bright,
Singing off-key, but what a delight!
His companions chuckle, they can't help themselves,
In this lyrical haven where laughter dwells.

Bees buzz around with a comedic flair,
Performing a dance without a care.
While the fish splash humor, creating a stir,
This landing of laughter is quite the cur.

So gather around for a splashy good time,
Enjoy the antics, the rhythm, the rhyme.
From frogs to ducks, every critter joins in,
In this lyrical landing, let the giggles begin!

Rhythmic Roots

Deep in the soil where the jokes do sprout,
Worms wiggle and laugh, there's no doubt.
A rhythmic dance, they twist and glide,
As beetles tap dance, filled with pride.

Squirrels gather, with nuts all around,
Trading puns that are truly profound.
The roots chime in, beneath the ground,
In this quirky rhythm, pure joy is found.

A gopher pops up, with a grin so wide,
Shares his puns with a side of pride.
Every critter contributes to the beat,
As laughter and music blend so sweet.

With every twist, and every turn,
The forest is filled with laughter to churn.
So dance with the roots, let your spirit break loose,
In rhythmic roots, find your joyous excuse!

The Fruits of the Forest

In the orchard where fruits take their stand,
Apples make faces, oh, isn't it grand?
Bananas chuckle with their silly peels,
While oranges roll, oh, how it feels!

Berries joke of their juicy fame,
As grapes get tangled, it's all the same.
The pear gives a wink, the plum joins the jest,
In this fruity fest, we are surely blessed.

A fig struts about with a nose up high,
Telling tales that might make you cry.
The forest is bursting with laughter and cheer,
As fruits keep you smiling, year after year.

So take a bite, let the fun ignite,
In the fruits of the forest, the mood is just right.
With every crunch and every sip,
Join the laughter, savor each quip!

Echoes of Nature's Song

The squirrel strums a tiny harp,
With acorns dancing all around.
A frog hops in with quite the bop,
While birds throw tunes from trees profound.

The wind joins in with gentle howls,
As rabbits tap their furry feet.
The grass provides soft laughing growls,
A chorus made for nature's beat.

A caterpillar hums along,
In sync with leaves that sway and sway.
The sun beams down, a bright-eyed throng,
As shadows play the game of day.

So let us sing, all creatures here,
In sync with nature's merry way.
For every sound, both loud and clear,
Is music that we love to play.

Deep in the Grove

In the grove where laughter grows,
A bear winks at a passing bee.
A turtle busts out epic prose,
While trees hold hands, all jubilee.

The mushrooms sport their polka dots,
Like fancy hats in grand parade.
The raccoons share the best thoughts,
While dancing under leafy shade.

Crickets chirp a witty tune,
As owls drop in for a chat.
The moon descends, a cheeky moon,
With glowing beams, all purrs and pat.

Oh, deep in the grove, joy is found,
With whirlwinds of fun swirling 'round.

Heartstrings of the Wilderness

In the wild, the heartstrings twang,
A fox plays tricks with a cawing crow.
The bear croons like a velvet fang,
While rabbits twist in a silly show.

Monkeys chuckle in the trees,
As raccoons steal a snack or two.
The river giggles in the breeze,
A bubbling chat, oh so askew!

Together, they weave a funny tale,
With every rustle, tweet, and leap.
From timid fawns to owls so pale,
They dance and tread, a secret keep.

The wilderness whispers, full of cheer,
A concert grand, when friends are near.

The Language of Leaves

The whispers of the leaves they tell,
Of gossip shared by bough and bud.
As breezes weave a leafy spell,
Laughing softly in their wood.

Each fluttering phrase, a playful jest,
From maple's giggles to oak's wise grin.
The wind scribbles poems in jest,
Inviting all to join in the din.

With foliage cheering, spirits soar,
While branches sway in a friendly fight.
The trees are wise but funny to the core,
In the dance of day that turns to night.

Thus, join the chat of leaves up high,
For every rustle holds laughter nigh.

Tuning into the Timber

In the forest where trees know how to dance,
   Saplings sway with a delightful prance.
   Squirrels giggle, their nuts on the run,
Branches chuckle, 'We're all just having fun!'

Moss on the ground, it jokes with the breeze,
   Tickling the toes of the bumblebee bees.
   Raccoons in crowns, sipping acorn tea,
Whispering secrets, oh, what glee they see!

   Under the canopy, shadows play chess,
Every move made earns a light-hearted mess.
The owls wear spectacles, reading the night,
Laughing so hard, they take flight in delight!

   Nature's symphony, a comedic shoot,
   Riffs from the branches, opinions to boot.
   Catch a good line, let it echo and chime,
In this vibrant world, we're all a good rhyme!

Serene Soil Sonnet

In the quiet dirt, the worms like to joke,
Throwing mud pies, oh what a poke!
Roses in giggles, shaking off dew,
While daisies debate whose hat is more blue.

Under the ground where the potatoes play,
Telling tall tales of the worms' funny way.
Carrots wear glasses, reading their fate,
Oh, the wise old radish thinks he's too late!

The compost heap's bubbling with laughter and cheer,
Telling the leaves, 'There's nothing to fear!'
With every green sprout, a chuckle will bloom,
In this garden of joy, there's always more room.

Soil full of humor, secrets it keeps,
Living life's antics while nature just sleeps.
In this patch of play, where nothing's a bore,
We'll sing to the roots, and ask, 'What's in store?'

Whimsy of the Wildflower

Wildflowers laugh as they tango with bees,
Tickling the petals, swaying with ease.
Dandelions shout, 'We're fluffy and free!'
While poppies blow kisses, a sight to see!

Buttercups bow, in their golden attire,
Sharing sweet secrets, they never tire.
With croaky old frogs that play leapfrog at night,
Pondering where the fireflies take flight.

The violets gossip, 'Do you see who's here?'
As startled grasshoppers jump with good cheer.
Their colorful petals a delightful show,
Making the meadow one grand, funny flow!

Under the sun, the blooms have their fun,
Every bright hue, a warm, silly pun.
In this giggling garden, where wildflowers cling,
Life's a merry dance, come join and sing!

Cellar of Sentiments

In the cellar where thoughts like to stew,
Dust bunnies giggle as they form a queue.
Old jars of pickles whispering tunes,
'Let's dance the night away, beneath the moons!'

Cobwebs do cartwheels, ignoring the dust,
While boots tell stories of adventures a must.
Bottles of laughter, vintage and fine,
Sipping on stories and passing the time.

The old trunk hums in a nostalgic way,
Bringing up memories from far away.
Lonesome old socks, they tap on the floor,
Adding rhythms to dreams they can't ignore.

In this quirky cellar, where the past starts to blend,
Every little anecdote gives way to a trend.
So raise up a toast, let the fun stories flow,
In our whimsical haunt, let the happy thoughts grow!

Threads of Past and Present

In a closet, secrets sway,
A sock with tales of yesterday.
It once was pair, now it's alone,
A lonesome life, a sad little tone.

Time spins yarns, oh what a sight,
A t-shirt claims it's still so bright.
Yet faded laughs drip from its seams,
Like distant echoes of wild dreams.

Grandma's dress, a dancing flare,
Worn at weddings, full of care.
Now it's just a fancy rag,
Where moths and memories do snag.

With every stitch, a laugh we find,
A thread of joy that's intertwined.
So let's wear our quirks and quirks,
For life's too short for stuffy shirts.

Rhyme's Embrace in Shadow

Around the corner, whispers play,
A garden gnome has gone astray.
He loiters near the fence so fine,
And giggles hard at every line.

The moonlight winks with every joke,
While shadows dance, a friendly bloke.
A melody hums in the night air,
As crickets chirp without a care.

They jest and prance, a merry lot,
Ushering dreams that can't be caught.
With laughter's bloom through every crack,
The stars nod softly, never slack.

So take a moment, join the jest,
For shadowed rhymes are simply best.
In giggles, find your reason why,
And let your laughter soar and fly.

The Understory of Emotion

Beneath the trees, where secrets twine,
A squirrel holds court as it dines.
It tosses nuts, a jest so grand,
While onlookers clap, a merry band.

Leaves rustle softly, sharing a tale,
Of a leaf with dreams, set to sail.
It drifts on whims, a whimsical dare,
Chasing the wind without a care.

Roots may tangle, but we laugh along,
For every twig hums a silly song.
The understory blooms with delight,
As critters frolic both day and night.

In tangled thoughts, emotions thrive,
While buds of joy dance to survive.
So gather 'round, let giggles bloom,
In nature's theater, there's always room.

Lyrics of Life and Leaf

Oh, the leaves, they sway and shimmy,
Whispering secrets, oh so whimsy.
Each crackle holds a funny twist,
A dance of life that can't be missed.

With every breeze, they sing and sway,
Reminding us to laugh today.
The lyrics penned with every fall,
Create a symphony through it all.

Life spins tales in colors bright,
A patchwork quilt of pure delight.
So let the laughter echo wide,
In nature's arms, let joy abide.

When absentminded thoughts arrive,
Just look to leaves—they're oh so alive.
Each rustle tells a joke or two,
In this leafy world, it's a comedy crew.

The Sound of the Soil

In the garden, worms hum tunes,
While daisies dance to afternoon swoons.
The carrots laugh beneath the ground,
Tickling roots with laughter profound.

Sunshine tickles the potatoes' skin,
As they gossip about where they've been.
With a wink, the radishes start to tease,
"Guess who'll make the best veggie cheese?"

Squirrels gather, wearing tiny hats,
Their chatter mixing with chit-chat of bats.
The beets giggle, rolling in glee,
"We're the best snacks for a tea party, you see!"

So soil sings with a whimsical cheer,
Nature's laughter rings crystal clear.
In this garden, let the fun bloom wide,
As the earthworms jive and the roots collide!

Hymn of the Horizon

Barley wakes with a stretch and a yawn,
Swaying gently like a sleepy fawn.
Corn whispers secrets in the breeze,
Telling tales of the nighttime trees.

The sunbeam tickles the greenest grass,
Rabbits hop by, threading like sass.
"Hey, did you hear? The clouds are late!"
They chuckle and bounce, feeling first-rate.

Stars twinkle down with a giggle or two,
As the moon's cheeky grin bids adieu.
The skyline's melody brings blissful cheer,
Nature's symphony we all hold dear.

Bumblebees buzz with a melodious swing,
Planting their laughter in every spring.
On the horizon, the fun takes flight,
As nature sings through the day and the night!

Tangle of Treetops

In a forest where branches lock and sway,
The squirrels debate who will win today.
"I'm the fastest!" yells one in a flare,
While another flips in midair with flair.

Leaves rustle laughter, a cheeky duet,
As the wind adds jokes we can't quite forget.
"Who needs a crown? I've got a branch!"
Cackles an owl, all ready to prance.

Twigs and vines weave a lively song,
Trees nodding along, where they all belong.
Each knot has a tale, each loop is divine,
In this tangled waltz, everything aligns!

Barks share giggles, roots give a cheer,
Moss claps along to the festivity near.
Every treetop knows in its leafy retreat,
That nature dances, and life is a treat!

Songs of the Silt

In a puddle silt sings soft and sweet,
"Watch out, there's a frog on my beat!"
The rushes giggle as the mud splashes,
While minnows twirl in delight as they dash.

"Have you heard the news? The rain's on its way!"
Chirps a snail, in his damp ballet.
"Let's throw a party, slugs bring the cake,
Eel can DJ, make the river shake!"

Tiny bubbles join in the fun,
While the sun peeks out, laughing at the run.
Even the cattails sway with a grin,
As they join in the muddy din.

Songs of the silt carry on a tune,
Celebrating life, morning to moon.
With nature's giggles, all worries cease,
In this underwater harmony, we find peace!

Verse of the Verdant

In gardens green, the laughter grows,
Where socks and shoes are lost in rows.
The daisies dance with goofy grace,
While bunnies hop, a silly race.

A toadstool's hat could host a show,
With jokes and jests from furry pro.
The gophers giggle, digging deep,
While ants form bands to sing and leap.

The carrots wear a jaunty grin,
As radishes join in the spin.
Oh, what a sight, this leafy crew,
With rhymes that sprout, oh how they grew!

So come and join the verdant fun,
Where every plant's a cheeky pun.
In soil and sun, let's laugh and play,
In this green realm, we'll joke all day.

Nestled in Verses

A squirrel recites his morning news,
While gathering up some playful foos.
With acorn hats and nutty jokes,
He entertains all woodland folks.

The trees sway gently to his beat,
As owls hoot rhymes from their lofty seat.
Each leaf a page that flutters by,
In echoes sweet of laughter high.

The brook joins in with giggly glee,
As pebbles bounce like they're set free.
A chorus of frogs, with voices loud,
Sing ballads bright, oh what a crowd!

Nestled in verses, they create,
A harmony that cannot wait.
So let us join this merry band,
In playful prose across the land.

Echoes of the Earth

Beneath the ground, where giggles dwell,
The worms tell tales they know so well.
In dirt they play, a messy game,
Forget the rules, all fun's the aim.

The rocks crack smiles and chuckle low,
As roots entwine, they steal the show.
With echoing laughter from below,
It's nature's joke, a fun tableau.

The mushrooms sprout in joyful lines,
With hats of polka dots like signs.
They twist and turn, a waltz of cheer,
In this earthy realm, there's naught to fear.

In echoes loud, the earth will sing,
Of hidden joys and playful things.
So dig right down, uncover mirth,
In laughter's depth, embrace the earth.

Whispers Beneath the Soil

A secret club of roots convenes,
To share their plans, their silly schemes.
With whispers soft and chuckles bright,
They plot their pranks beneath the night.

The trowels dream of grand parades,
Where daisies wear their finest shades.
And radishes with ruffled ends,
Convene with carrots, laughing friends.

The earthworms write a comedic play,
With puns that twist and twist all day.
They wriggle 'round to hear the cheer,
As laughter bubbles up near here.

In whispers low, the soil hums,
With joy that springs from silly drums.
In every clod, a giggle waits,
In nature's heart, the humor states.

Tangles of Time and Tone

In a garden where clocks all chime,
A squirrel holds court with a rhyme.
Tangled in tunes of the past,
He begs for a snack, but it's gone too fast.

The daisies dance with their heads held high,
While the crickets all jump and fly.
They laugh as they jump over sunbeam,
And toss silly shadows, oh what a dream!

A snail is now throwing a bash,
With gossip and jokes, it's quite the smash.
While frogs sing tunes in the muddy heap,
They promise you laughter, but never sleep.

So if you stumble on this merry spree,
Join the fun, grab a cup of glee.
For time is just laughter that hops and squats,
Tangled in jests and all the silly thoughts.

Seeds of Sonnetry

I tossed my words into the breeze,
They sprouted up through giggling trees.
A sunflower wore a silly hat,
And asked me why I sat like that.

The bumblebees buzzed a jazzy tune,
While tulips played cards from noon to moon.
I lost my seeds in a game of chance,
Now daisies are trying to do the dance!

They waltz on the grass with all their might,
While worms debate what's wrong or right.
In this garden of verbal delight,
Every rhyme takes flight in pure delight!

So join the blooms, and spin your tale,
As pansies tell jokes that never fail.
In this patch of giggles, let's take flight,
Sowing the laughter from morning till night.

The Pulse of Nature's Lyric

A robin croons a silly song,
While ants march in a line so long.
They chant of cupcakes and sunny days,
So celebrate in these wacky ways!

Breezes tickle the leaves and sway,
As trees make faces, bright and gay.
With laughter sprouting from roots below,
Nature's chorus puts on quite a show!

The flowers giggle when clouds roll by,
As they trade puns with a nearby fly.
In this realm of rhyme, we find our groove,
Each note a chuckle that makes us move.

So let us dance where the wild things hum,
In the pulse of nature, we all become;
A melody of mirth, an earthen delight,
As we sway to the rhythms of day and night.

Grown from the Ground

From soil deep, the laughter blooms,
Tickling toes as sunlight looms.
The carrots cracking all the jokes,
While cabbages dance like silly folks.

On leafy greens the shadows play,
As radishes giggle and sway.
They whisper secrets to turns of fate,
While pumpkins ponder on their weight!

A cabbage goes 'round like a wobbly king,
Declaring that laughter is the best thing.
With marigolds chuckling, all is right,
In this patch of joy, we take our flight.

So come all ye creatures, gather 'round,
Join the parade of fun we found.
In this garden of giggles, let us sow,
A crop of laughter that continues to grow!

Stanzas of the Forest

In the woods where trees wear hats,
Squirrels dance like acrobats.
Rabbits hop and giggles soar,
The forest floor, a laugh galore!

Fungi munch on shadows' dreams,
While sunlight sprinkles golden beams.
Owls wink with mischievous glee,
Whispering secrets to the bee.

Branches sway in silly style,
While chipmunks cheer and share a smile.
Nature's jesters, filled with cheer,
Make the woodland feel so near!

In this place where laughter grows,
Life's a game of tickle toes.
Among the leaves, a comic scheme,
In every nook, a jolly dream!

Rhythms of the Roots

Beneath the ground where whispers thread,
Worms host parties, overhead.
They jig and jive in muddy hues,
While dancing with the funky cues.

Mice in tuxedos roll and twirl,
Fungi rock, in earth's big whirl.
Roots they tap, a lively beat,
Jiving close, in rhythmic feet.

Grubs play drums with acorn caps,
Echoing laughter, silly claps.
Underneath, the giggles bloom,
Nature's joy, a vibrant room!

Swaying softly in the dirt,
Silly secrets, never curt.
Feeling free and full of cheer,
In this hidden world so dear!

The Harmony of the Harvest

Veggies gather, what a scene,
Carrots grinning, oh so keen.
Tomatoes blush and dance around,
In the patch, joy's always found!

Basil twirls in fragrant spins,
While peppers giggle, wearing grins.
Radishes joke in modest peeks,
Chortling through their rosy cheeks.

Corny puns on every cob,
Cucumbers play their garden mob.
With every breeze, a playful shout,
These harvests never wear out!

As the sun sets low and red,
Fruity frolics fill their head.
Nature's comedy, ripe and free,
A bountiful laugh in harmony!

Underground Sonnet

Deep below, where shadows prance,
Moles conduct a secret dance.
With shovels made of tiniest claws,
They chuckle at the dirt and flaws.

Earthworms twist in goofy loops,
Throwing parties with the goops.
To the beat of silent hums,
They share a laugh and eat resplendums.

Roots recite the silliest jokes,
While critters cheer like jovial folks.
Gophers wink from burrowed beds,
Dreaming of fanciful breads.

In this soil, a jest so grand,
Crickets sing with a merry band.
Under earth, where smiles creep,
Life's absurd, but oh, so deep!

www.ingramcontent.com/pod-product-compliance
Lightning Source LLC
Chambersburg PA
CBHW051656160426
43209CB00004B/925